Love in my Language

Book II

For my little Bunni.

Love will make you
lose yourself and
find yourself in the same breath.

Author's Note

This journey has been an exploration of self. It's been two years since I've started writing again and a little over a year since I've shared my words publicly. Personally, I have witnessed growth from the inside out and it has been humbling. I found my language and love in the same place, which I never thought was possible. When writing, I often ask myself, "Are you being honest?" If I can't answer yes I put my pen down. I've found that as a young writer, who has a story to tell, it's imperative that I am telling my truth in its rawest form. If I am not, that takes away from the art, from the love and from the language. I do not want to sell my writing short by being fearful of my truth. In these pages you will find pieces of me scattered. Unlike my previous book, "Words from a Wanderer," this collection of work will give you an in depth look at my darkness and the discovery of my light. My hope is that "Love in my Language" will be received with open hearts and minds.

Welcome to my story.

With Love,

Alex Elle

Find Your Language

Writings

Find Your Language

Poetry

Open

I am still coming to terms with my past and the truth is I know hurt like the back of my hand. The same hurt that left emotional welts on my spirit came with healing. No matter how broken we may seem to be, we are never too shattered to put our peace back together.

I will never forget the day that my daughter's father blatantly told me "I would never have any more kids with you. You and your family have funny genes." As I write this, years later, my heart still manages to sink to my feet. That alone was the most hurtful thing I had heard and I've heard some things.

I think my daughter was five months or so when the reality of my situation kicked in. I wanted a family, foolishly with someone who didn't love me, I wanted more children with someone who didn't see beauty when they looked at me. My self-esteem was already nonexistent and at that point my worth was shot and damned to hell.

I had to start asking myself some serious questions. There was a reason why I was so comfortable with staying in dysfunction. In reality I was the only person who could really figure out why. Even my therapist, who helped me a lot, could not give me the ultimate answers. I avoided having my self talk for a long time but the realization that my truth could not be avoided became louder each day. Why at age 18 did I sign up to parent a child with someone who was just as lost as I was? How could we raise a child with one another when we were strangers to each other's real world?

Why was my worth buried within another human being so deeply? If I knew then what I know now many things would be different. But on my journey to self realization and preservation, I've learned this:

Know better. Do better. Love better.

No one, not a baby or a man, could give me the light of self worthiness. Overtime that lesson became loud and clear, and I will always keep that with me.

When I look back on things now it was clear that we were both so young and different spaces. I was stuck between wanting to stay and wanting to change. He was seemingly just stuck but other people's battles are not ours to take on. We would force talks about marriage and love when both of us knew that was not what we truly desired. However the truth always comes to light with time.

I recall him saying that he would never marry me in this lifetime. We were so different and still are. Our views were not the same and we were in no way "equally yoked." Day by day I realized that I was not only not good enough for him but also not for myself. I constantly felt inferior and ashamed for being who I was. Our differences were transparent in many ways but I intentionally avoided to see things for what they were.

He made it a point to stress he hoped that our baby had pretty hair while I was hoping that she had a good heart. We were opposites; oil and water in a way.

The relationship was so unhealthy, and looking back on it now, I can see things extremely clear. The hurtful and emotionally abusive moments are still so vivid. I hated him and he hated me. There was no love, not the real kind. At the time I wish we knew how to love in a way that didn't hurt. Through it all my

2

daughter has been my life's biggest blessing but under all of the beauty I now live in, I had a lot of healing to do.

I have been ripped open.

I know what it's like to be unwanted.

I am familiar with the un-pretty feelings we are sometimes greeted with in the mirror.

I was seeking and longing for something nonexistent from someone I didn't really know. Being lost was an understatement—I had literally died or so I thought. After my daughter was born life got dark for me. I spent days in my room with the windows blocked off. My depression had gotten a hold of me; I wasn't eating and my body showed the world that it was starving. I was cutting again while trying to produce enough breast milk to feed my baby. I was at a turning point and would soon be tested by God. He'd see me succeed even when I wanted to succumb to being broken. I remember sitting on my bed thinking of ways to hang myself from my door when my mom walked in with my baby. We sat and we cried. My momma told me that my storm was passing and to please hold on. I was so tired of being misguided by my insecurities.

Things got better but it took a long time and a lot of effort on my part. The biggest lesson I have learned in my life is that we are never alone in our struggle. The rain will stop and your rainbow will shine bright.

You will be victorious.

You are triumphant.

Find love in yourself.

I think we all forget about ourselves at times.

I have to learn to remember me.

- Mindful

Patient

I try to be patient with people but sometimes I forget to be patient with myself. My heart is open and accepting of others but sometimes I am not capable of returning that love to myself. After years of feeling inadequate it's very hard for me to not second guess my choices. So many people will never understand that about me.

I've been talked out of things. I've been judged and emotionally abused in relationships, so there are days where I feel like I am not good enough for anyone.

My growth has taken a lot of self-reflection and to say the least it's been eye opening. I try my best to work on not giving up or going backwards, even on the days when I am feeling stuck. I have moments of feeling unworthy but I have to remind myself, on my not so sunny days, that I am worth all of the goodness that comes my way.

I will build patience by:

When you reach for me, reach with love. I vow to return your extension with open arms and a dancing heart.

- **Rhythm**

Here

I never thought I'd be one for long distance love. I tried it and failed at it before so I laid it to rest. My past interest wasn't here and when I say "here" I don't mean physically.

I don't want you if you're not present in my life; if you're not "here" with me I will ask you to leave. I stand tall today in love with a man that is three-thousand miles away. I can feel him here despite the distance. He is present and active in my life. He is a part of my everyday all the way from across the country.

I believe in love because of people like him; people who are present, aware and interested in loving me how I love them. It's such a beautiful feeling. It's a real feeling that is unmatched.

I met him at a good time, in a good place. We complement one another and even though he's not physically here, he is "here" and that's what most important.

Sometimes I don't want to share.

Sometimes I just don't have the energy in me to give.

I want to be selfish and

wrap

up

in myself

with no explanation as to why.

- Selfish

Sunflower

He remembered that I love sunflowers.

I smiled as I followed the petals up the steps and through the doorway- there he stood with love in his eyes, gazing at me with just the stem...

My heart stopped and my eyes welled up with tears, watching his lips slowly part to speak, I saw just how beautiful he was. "Will you follow me to the sun?" he asked. "Will you pick up the petals I left for you and adhere them back to the stigma of this stem because I would for you. I'd walk a million miles for your heart. I would collect every flower that blooms in the spring and I'd hand them to you one by one until your arms could cradle no more." At that moment he was my center, the balance I've been longing to attain. I replied quietly, "I will be your moon should you allow me that honor..." while falling to my knees, consumed with joy, I began to collect the petals he had left for me. I planned to strategically place every last piece of yellow back on the center of my sunflower's stem.

I won't forget where I love from.

- Roots

Flexibility

We are all a work in progress. No one really knows everything that their friends and family have been through, gone through or are going through at this present moment. A lot of us have different defense mechanisms in attempts to protect our hearts and feelings. However, many times those defense moves can sabotage relationships. For me, I have trust issues that stem from a lot of different things.

My way of coping is to remove people from my space. I am protective of my sanity and feelings, but I also try to avoid conflict that can cause hatred and distaste. Taking a step back has kept me calm, cool and collected for the most part. Although shifting space is good for my sake, I rarely take into consideration how my abrupt distance could make someone else feel, despite the closeness of our relationship. Over the past few months I have been doing a lot of reflecting. I was told by a very close friend of mine that, "You have to learn to be flexible or you will break. It's not all or nothing every single time." She was right.

It's not always the other person more so than it is us and our baggage from past experiences. I have no reservations about the people that I truly trust in my heart.

When my heart is certain, it's easy to be free and open with them about everything. However I am learning that I do not hold everyone close to me in the same regard. With that being the case, I've had to figure out why I rather remove people from my life versus trying to work through rough patches. Is it me or them?

Sometimes we need to take a hard look in the mirror and make changes. Making strides to be better requires care and effort all across the board not just in one area of life.

My greatest lesson in learning flexibility is this:

You shouldn't hold other people accountable for how someone else has treated you in the past. Cherish your relationships and build trust by communicating open and honestly.

Don't ruin great things because you're stuck on how things were or are with other people in your life.

Everyone is not the same or out to hurt you.

Be flexible or prepare to break in half.

I will be flexible by:

The Gift of Light

I saw the moon out last night; she was dancing beautifully,
lighting up the sky with a subtle kiss of white.

I met a king not too long ago and he was lonely.

His jewels weren't enough, his silver and gold will soon tarnish
from neglect and his heart is a stranger to love.

Some nights my heart crumbles into pieces from the loneliness
that echoes through the sky.

Witnessing two beautiful beings living alone, dancing alone
and with no one to love or nurture was stifling.

The King looks at me with love in eyes but still will not come
close enough for me to touch him.

I decided to give him a gift; a gift that couldn't be replaced
even if it was deemed tangible. I plucked the dancing moon
from her bed of stars, wrapped her in a bow and left her on the
King's doorstep where she brilliantly glowed.

Now he won't be alone; they can dance together and be together
even in the darkest of times.

Maybe he will learn to love her and enjoy the light she brings
to his life...

Or maybe it'll be me that he thinks of when he lays his head
down at night.

And if the sun was to crash from the sky I would not run from it; instead I would stand atop its flames and melt into its glory.

- Absorb

The Battle

I was convinced that my pain flowed through my bloodstream. The sharp edge was my friend; kissing each one of my veins like a speeding train on broken tracks. How to rid the horror and hurt, the hate and horrendous feeling of existing? My mind tricked me into cutting it out. Blade to my brown skin, bloodied and hopeless — I walked around with scars that only made me feel more insecure. I'd be sitting there, Indian style, watching my tears pour into my open wounds. The stinging sensation of sin was the only way I knew that I was still alive. Bracelets and watches couldn't hide the damage and I was too proud to walk around bandaged. I was impatiently waiting for my floor to cave in and hug me to hell. I wanted to collapse from the cutting but I couldn't; my cuts weren't deep enough. Or maybe my tool wasn't sharp enough. Perhaps God was convinced that I hadn't lived long enough to change the world. To me, that thought was unfathomable. I was just another daddy-less black girl who has fallen victim to the ways of the world.

I guess I was wrong because I am still standing.

I was kept alive and breathing on my bathroom floor while swimming in sorrow at sixteen. Drip drop went the blood drops that painted the linoleum hiding underneath me.

And now at twenty-four, I stare at my daughter and smile with joy. Eight years later, I gaze in the mirror and say "look at me."

I am not afraid of my truth anymore and I will not omit pieces of me to make you comfortable.

- **Honest**

It's hard enough that I have to write them down when
I can barely spit them out.
Being tongue tied has helped me realize that a lot of
things still hurt.

- Feelings

Heightened Senses

Senses erect from the stroke of the wind, I take you in...

I cradle your breath in dip of my neck as I spin in circles of love around you. Enticed by how much you adore my every motion, those circles turn into piquès...

You keep me on my toes and I don't need to be classically trained in ballet to know that you are my relevè.

Your lip prints make my skin rise; you keep me lifted beyond sky high and I let you peacefully come down and drown in my ocean of passion.

I do not wonder or even think to ask why because you're my darling who I adore with every vein within my vessel. My right hand, my right brain you can have both if in return it's you I gain. I've learned your smile.

The laugh you expel is mesmerizing and the way your eyelashes kiss in between blinks of infatuation makes me believe in God.

There are certain little things that I will never forget.

You told me that my goose bumps tell you stories as your fingertips outline the curves in the arch of my back...

Senses erect from the touch of your being, I take you in but this time I will hold my breath, exhaling is not an option.

I'm human.

I'm not perfect...

and sometimes I don't know better.

- Learning

Continue

Some days you are going to feel like the world is against you. There will be times when you think no one understands your struggles or your passion.

When you reach points like this in your journey try your best to keep a clear mind; negative thoughts are fleeting. Stay focused and driven. Pursue your dreams, love your life.

Not everyone is going to understand or support your life walk. As long as you keep sight of your end goal you will continue stepping forward to greatness.

I will continue to:

I will not change the rhythm of my heartbeat to accommodate men who do not understand her song.
She sounds beautiful and deserves to be heard with open ears.

-Worthy

Happy

Sometimes you have to be still, be silent and greet adversity with love. It's important that we find balance and comfort in what we gain and lose. I used to have a very hard time letting people go and letting people in. It seemed as though every time I let someone in, soon after I found myself separating myself from them.

Whether it was a romantic or platonic relationship, I always chose me first. I can't be great for people who are bad for me and I had to learn that I needed to stop chasing after relationships that were fading. Some things are worth the fight but others are not. Learning the difference was essential for my growth. For many years I thought I was being selfish but soon realized that my happiness lies within me. If the company I was keeping didn't bring light to that happiness they had to go. Protecting your "happy" isn't selfish and you shouldn't feel bad about taking precautions to do so. If you know in your heart that you are a good person, you should surround yourself with goodness—whatever or whoever that may be.

My happy is:

I've learned to say "no." I can't be everything to everyone else if I am nothing to myself.

-The N word

If I (An Extension of Gratitude)

If I wrote a letter to my father it would simply ⌐ ⌐
you." The two words that have taken me years to muster up
will read with ease in the hand written note.

The thanks would render gratitude for leaving me behind, for
the broken promises and not so good behaviors that I picked up
from his scattered presence. "Thank you" would be his present
for barely being present; and now since I am older I hold his
inconsistent lessons close. I picked a good man because of
him. He would be thanked for indirectly teaching me what not
to look for in a man and what not to stand for as a woman. It's
been a long time coming but thanks would be given for
being a liar.

Without his deception I would not know what the truth looked
like. I would say "thank you" for letting me down and for
coincidentally teaching me how to forgive those who have
wronged me.

And if I were feeling wordy I would say: It's not your fault
that I was broken; you didn't know how to fix yourself, so
how could you know how to repair me? Your ignorance did
not translate into bliss but it birthed a blessing. Thank you for
being deceitful, hurtful and damaged. I've learned so much
by watching you fail. So much so, that one day, after emerging
from my darkness, I grew wings and started to fly. You are not
to blame anymore for my pieces.I've taken my power back and
my peace is plentiful.Thank you for knowing no better because
from that alone I've learned a lot.

Let me be your wild flower.

I want to root my love into your heart and stay there until

we blossom into something unseen

by the masses.

Our garden will be beautiful

and just for us to tend to.

- Glory

Warmth

Your warmth is reminiscent of sunshine on a cool autumn day. You know the kind you stand in for a few seconds just to shake the chill?

I can still feel your fingertips tracing the ridges of my noir colored tank top that I bought from Target over the summer. It's my favorite and now I may not ever wash it. That night, if you really wanted to, you could've heard my heart sing but you weren't listening close enough, she was putting on a show. Barely spooning and not close enough to fit in that pocket underneath your arm but I'll admit that while you were talking, I was counting each exhale you took to speak. I wish you peace and wellness, happiness and joy—for no other reason but to thank you for being you. I like your smile and your mind, your laugh and the way your denim fits. Your warmth is reminiscent of something greater than you will ever know...

What makes you warm?

Maybe I love you because you ring the love out of my heart. Or, maybe, I love you because you count my flaws as perfections created by God.

- **Imperfections**

Writer Love

Writer love has its moments — they aren't always brilliant but indeed passionate. Writers know what to say and how to say it, when to say it and how to put it so eloquently so that you may fall in love from the slightest breath of them. The whisper of a writer is perfection in it purest form.

Being a writer, I can say this with no hesitation.

The poet in me fools people sometimes but the lover in me is genuine and yielding, humbled but not always forgiving.

I think writers scare each other. We fall fast and things can end just as quickly as they begin. In our moments written together bliss is produced even if it's perfection for just one second. I've learned a lot about myself, specifically within this past year. Meeting a fellow poet, kissing him, making love with him, and sharing space on his college ruled pages was electrifying but our light dwindled slowly. Our passion went away and my love wasn't enough to secure a permanent spot in his notebook. I didn't know him, I knew his words. His actions were far and in between but I let my heart love him anyway, just because in that split second, I felt it was worth giving a try. It's not good to fall in love with words. Me of all people should have known that seemingly beautiful things aren't always authentic, I taught myself that years ago.

I don't regret our moments, words, phrases or even our silence. He taught me things about me. He was my muse. My notepad is full of writing inspired by his being; that writer love was temporarily impeccable.

If I didn't let my heart love him I wouldn't have pages of greatness to revisit. I just wish we talked more and wrote less sometimes. During moments of conflict we would take to our notepads and pour out our emotions there; his about how he couldn't love me and mine about how I loved him too much. We never talked but I think we both realized that we can't just write our problems away. Even when we ripped out the pages and started over, the problems still remained. Being with a writer was beautiful but draining. Lovely but heartbreaking simultaneously and sadly my heart will forever beat for him. That's what happens with writers, we fall in love and can't shake it so we write about it until we force ourselves to hate them — that energy is only for a moment though. Writer love doesn't just go away, even though our passion couldn't outweigh our truth. Being with a writer has its perks but we can't promise to love you back. However, we can guarantee to create you the best run on sentence you've ever read. I know it's unfair. It'll make you think we care more than we are really capable of caring.

After a while you'll want a real apology for the lack of love, instead of a poem that's used to make up for past mistakes. Eventually, those writer's love words won't be enough to keep you happy. Sometimes I wanted to rip that journal he used because it knew everything about him that he wasn't willing to tell me. It knew things about me that I didn't even know he took note of. I'm a writer who fell in love with another writer's words; those beautiful words. A poet fooled me.

A writer used me and I still love him for giving me those moments of false perfection. Writer love is accidentally difficult if you aren't apart of the same genre or familiar with a similar pen stroke. We are the most loving, truthful, sugar coating, and unpredictable, inattentive, forgetful, passionate, driven and chaotic people on this earth.

Writers are different and loving one isn't always in the best interest of a partner unequipped to handle our plethora of beauty. Take it from me.

Wrap me in your mouth; tell me the truth about who you are and how you love with your tongue.

- French Kiss

Honesty Hour

Honestly, I don't really know what I'm doing.
Half of the time I'm just as confused as everyone else who is
walking in circles and struggling to catch their breath. I'm
a hopeless romantic who has trouble hiding the fact that I'm
extremely transparent. You can see my truth if you look hard
enough. My heart has been broken so I try not to overwork
her. People I love have vanished and a lot of the time I feel as
if I'm standing alone. I comfort myself with the words of my
poems; I drown in my own zone. Most nights, I don't sleep...
I rather be underdressed than overrated. My personality is
vibrant, paired with a sharp tongue and bad temper but I'm
learning to turn my fire down and allow my soul to simmer.
I'm a cry baby and a tad bit selfish but I'm relentlessly
honest about who I'm called to be even if the girl in the
mirror isn't who I want to see. I walk alone on a slightly
wider road because I tend to wander... I've been guilty of
backtracking and I've tripped a few times forward.
I'm blinded by what I'm looking for and I enjoy the rain from
indoors. I don't apologize for my feelings because they give
me character and poise. My pride keeps me quiet and I second
guess my purpose often. I could care less if my clothes match
because they don't reflect my heart...
Honestly, I don't really know what I'm doing.
Half the time I'm just as confused as everyone else.

Skin the color of love itself.

She finally learned to love herself.

-Transparent

I was made to love you.

I was made to love, period.

There's no mistaking the love we've created.

You've splashed my life with vibrant colors; this love is brighter than the rainbows that are birthed from the storms of tomorrow.

I was made to love.

I was made to love you, period.

I will color your heart with joy and leave it dancing for more.

I will love you forever, all ways always.

-Colorful

Kiss me;

choke on my stars so that I can light your soul on fire.

- Contagious

I love seeing:

Black men who undeniably love black women and not just for
our curves, color combinations, thickness, lips and breasts
but because of our honey, our flavor, our sweetness, our poise
and the loudness of our souls. They see us as Queens; they
crown us as such. It is understood that we can be modestly
grandiose; even though some may claim our blackness leaves
us ashamed and scared to show our God given glow.

I melt seeing:

Black men who undeniably love black women for birthing their
daughters and raising their sons and who embrace that fact that
we are not just a vessel or a beautiful bold statue to show off.
We are where they come from, we are who they love.

-Black Men (Undeniable Love)

He fell in love with a writer, bless his heart.

He will now be her haiku, ghazal and ode forever.

There will be no end with him as her beginning.

I almost feel sorry for him and her pen...

-Muse

I'm going to love you.

Whether you love me back or not is up to you.

-No Pressure

Trust

Believe that when you can't have something now you're being prepared for something greater later.

Timing is everything.

You can't rush your garden to grow.

Your life will be fruitful in due time; and with hard work you will reap the love that you sow. Beautiful things come to us when we accept who we are, where we are and how God is working. Wait it out, your turn is near.

Fall for someone who deserves to catch you.

-Belong

Daddy Issues: 1

I want to be able to love freely; with no attachments
but I always seem to get stuck to them like glue.
Detaching is like ripping an old band aid from sensitive skin.
I blame my father.

Gentle Reminder: 1

Don't confuse protecting your heart with being too scared to try something new with someone else, there is a difference. A lot of us have given way too much power to our pasts. Not everyone who may want a chance is going to use that chance against you negatively. Yes, some folks may fool us, trick us and even hurt us but some is not all. Don't miss out on a good thing because your past is persuading you not to pursue your future.

I do not feel empty when we part but whole.

Replenished but not full; I can never get enough of you.

- **Fix**

The Gifted

There are people here on earth who will never understand you. They won't get your passion and they'll mistake your drive with just a dream that you'll never be able to grasp. The beauty in their doubt is the ability to make them watch you stumble your way to the top with or without them. Trust me, they will be watching and waiting for you to fall. However, you will never come crashing down because your drive to succeed isn't just a dream, it's your reality. What I have learned over the years is that what is mine will always be mine. My gifts aren't for others to "get" or understand. My life walk is captivating, even to the ones who are determined to see me burn where I stand.

My gifts are:

At a young age I started ripping myself open just to
see what was inside.
I guess I was simply trying to find myself.

-Discovery

I once thought that love looked like something extravagant.
It was rare that I took into consideration that love could be
presented as something simple like a smile or a kind hello.
When I stopped loving to simply get love back, things became
clear and I felt at peace.
Be open to love no matter the capacity.
If it's genuine and has the potential to change even a little bit
of your life that should be more than welcomed too.

 -Simple

There's so much beauty in getting still and being quiet.
Practice finding peace from within.

-Meditate on Love

Its 2am and all I can think of is reaching out

and

touching you.

The outline of your shadow is etched

in my mind

but

when I rise to reach for you, your silhouette fades

into the night.

You make me realize every night what I am missing.

-Yearning

Loving freely is so much more than giving away the goodness that you have in your heart. It's also learning how to accept the bad, the ugly and the unfairness that you might be greeted with as you give your love away.

-Free Love

There's no art to being in love.

You don't need to lose your breath to feel it or mend your heart to know it.

-Second Nature

I told myself I wasn't gonna' write about you anymore
but my notepad is calling your name.
So, I guess, there's no escaping you.
I write in pen so there's no erasing you.
You are welcomed warmly here on these pages.

-Diary

Daddy Issues: 2

I eat men.

I spit them out.

I break their hearts because my daddy broke mine.

It's only right, right?

I run from them.

They are wanted but not welcomed here.

My mother tried her best, she blames my father.

Thank you for being who I thought you weren't.

You taught me something.

-Lesson Learned

If you'd like to leave this place, this space, then do so quietly.

Please do whatever it is you need to do to preserve your happy, to keep you safe.

I will blatantly cheer for your sanity.

I hope leaving gives you clarity...

But please do not flee out of fear or just to get a taste of what it is out there without me.

This world will not win, and when you decide to return, my door will be locked and you will not be allowed to enter back in.

-The Point of No Return

It's not who I am to you but who I am to me.

I know me well...

-Sense of Self

What does light look like?

How does it feel?

Maybe it's the sun colliding into the moon at noon

or

could it be the dark starless sky?

Either way, I see your light.

I feel it when you look my way.

I don't need to experience the sunrise to know that you are a

radiant part of my cloudiest days.

-Definition

I don't want someone who is looking to mold me or repair the damage done.

I want someone to love me for who I am.

-I'm Not Broken

I sought out Peace.

I found her; she told me that I needed boundaries.

She was right.

I have put up a fence with a gate and a lamp pole.

It's beautiful and white and covered in flowers that travel from one side to the other.

If my flame is not lit, you may not come in.

-I Call Her Peace

Yes, I want you here but I love me more.

Keep in mind that you are just a visitor.

You are not allowed to bring your baggage into my space and simply leave it.

-Tidy

Please keep in mind that no one can love you as much as you do. If you fall in love with yourself first, flaws and all, you will be able to exude beauty, kindness and love to others. There are too many instances where we expect to find our love in someone else. Look inside yourself for adoration, confidence and esteem. You owe yourself the love that you so freely give to other people.

-The Love in You

I wish I had the words in my mouth to describe what
I feel for you.
I feel for you; your goose bumps are my braille
and my taste buds hold your name on the tip of my tongue.

-Love Language

Likeness

There's always beauty within us despite if others acknowledge it or not. True beauty will radiate regardless. It's not your duty to remove the blinders of those who choose not to see you. You are equipped with your truth and no one can snatch that.I've had people lie on me and love on me.

I quickly learned that with the bad always comes the good. It took me years to see things that way. No matter what I've gone through I've realized that light illuminates light; and from the true light of our souls love reflects back at us.

Having someone who loves me because that's what their heart wants is a beautiful thing. I will never coax anyone to lay their love here.

-Authentic

His name gets caught in the pit of my belly, in the small of
my back and on the tip of my tongue. I don't remember giving
him the rights to my heart this way, and anyway, who said he
could stay here? He weaves his love in and out of my spirit like
he belongs here. I'm imprinted, my soul is lifted and dammit
it feels good. He might as well be tattooed somewhere on me
because it's visible that this isn't just a thing, it's permanent.
I just wish I knew how to love back, like really love back...
I can't even say his name because it's stuck in vocal cords that
have been shredded by premature "I love you's" and such.

-Incapable

He held her close to his left side.

It's almost like she belonged in his chest.

-Heartbeat

I want to give him children.

He has my permission to plant his seeds in fertile soil.

I've surrendered to one.

Love we will make, a chance we will take to recreate greatness.

My womb is reserved for his beauty, his blessing; and together we will come to give thanks to the most high.

Glory.

I want to carry his flowers, nurture them and feed them until they bloom...

Until I can hold them in my hands, love we will make.

-Make Love

I reach for him in my sleep

and rise daily with our dream in my hands.

-Reality

Getting a piece of me should not require you wanting me to break.

-Share

My feelings cascade down the arch of my back beautifully.

The beginning of my being is carried up my

spine leaving me numb to what I used to know; I am a woman.

-Standing Tall

Removing the Noise

Sometimes nothing is louder than my silence. I have found myself in the depths of my quiet plenty of times and my nothingness is now reflected back to me as beautiful. During the hush of my alone time, the hum of my heart is what really resonates with me. The silence hasn't always been great or by choice but it's always been good for me. Quiet is the food for my soul and the answer to all of my questions. As I have journeyed there have been moments of failure and fragility, but each time that I have stumbled, I'm picked back up by my truth. Stillness has never left me bruised and battered — soundlessness has freed me; it's made me whole and new.

How will you quiet down?

I belong to no one but myself.

Know better, do better, love better.

-Realization

How perfect aren't you?

That's what I really want to know.

-Do Tell

Valued Lesson

When I understood that forgiveness does not mean re-entry
I was able to find peace. Forgiving someone does not always
equal, "come back here; please stay." Sometimes forgive means
sending others on their way gently. Having a forgiving heart
will help to heal your stinging wounds. Being able to forgive
another without harboring ill feelings takes trust; trust in
yourself that things may happen but nothing can truly harden
the heart.

There is a love here that
cannot be broken or stolen.
I had to put up a fight with my own reflection to take back
what belonged to me.

-Belongings

And I told myself, "There will always be love here for you; even when you're depleted and empty."

-Abundant

A woman's worth does not nestle in between her legs
and it can't be found around the shape of her backside.
A woman's worth is not glorified in her cup size, hair length,
eye color or skin tone...
You cannot just walk up a woman's thigh with your fingertips
and see her soul through her womb—you can't truly know her
worth by simply exploring her physically.
A woman's worth is carried in her mental, in the glow of her
spirit and shine of her smile...
Her worth cannot be groped or mishandled, abused or
misguided—it is too solid to be broken down yet too fragile to
just be thrown away...
A woman's worth is protected but her kindness and emotional
flexibility to stand un-swayed and deeply rooted during her
stormiest days.

-What Some Don't Say

My words are meant to cut you open.

I hope they leave you sore and fragile with welts of love.

- Evidence

I'd like a man with hair on his face,

pride on his back

and a love in his eyes that has my name on it.

-King

I am a Leo;

born in the seventh month on the twenty-fifth day.

The Gods call me fiery.

My heart swells with love but in an instant can explode into
flames. The tongue I hold inside is sharp and has spewed
words that have cut deep. I am proud to say that I have dulled it
down.

-Lioness

Valuable

I was once afraid to let goodness greet me. When something or someone good would come my way I would run from the blessing. My heart wasn't open to receive and my mind was convinced that I wasn't "really" worthy. I was living in fear instead of walking in faith. I missed out on a lot because I was too scared to see what was really in front of me. When I opened my eyes and arms to the goodness that was waiting for me, things changed. I became encouraged to try and less afraid of failing. I now embrace the fact that everything isn't meant to be a walk in the park and just because that is so, it doesn't mean I'm not allowed to experience, accept and enjoy what is meant for me.

If I could love you once I'd do it again 10 times over.

-Permission

Stop loving in circles.

You're making your heart dizzy.

-Love Sick

I love how gentle you are while handling my heart...

How you glaze me with a love that is fragrant and soft, calm and reminiscent of something I've never had-you are easily my favorite scent. My most enjoyed everything; there is nothing better than your warmth. You're the definition of comfort, you remind me of home.

-Familiar

Your aroma lingers along my spine from the kisses you
leave behind; subtle but sweet.

It's like I'm waiting to be cut open and exposed when your
lips leave my melanin but I am not ashamed of the seeds that
trickle out of my flesh because they are yours to sow.

I add you to everything, you are the piece of me that
I never knew existed...

You bring back the memories of happiness from my younger
days when everything was innocent and pure.

-Vanilla Bean and Love

I seek refuge in actions and comfort in words.

Thank you for making your heart my home.

I value the table setting of love that you've arranged for us, you are where I belong.

-Shelter

Journey

When I found myself...

I think I was laying in bits and pieces on my bedroom floor, which was flooded with tears and heartache. My truth had been carved into my wall with pieces from my shattered mirror that I couldn't bear to face on a daily basis. What was wrong with me? Where had I been all this time? Where on earth was I going? Jogging in circles had gotten so tiring; I was worn out. All I remember about my old self was the need for a man to love me more than my father did. My entire worth was wrapped up in being good enough for someone else instead of being amazing for myself. I wanted to be worthy enough to stay with but everyone always left. Day by day I convinced myself that love didn't live here and it definitely didn't love me how I loved it. When push came to shove, I was moving way too fast in a world that never stands still. Going through that heartache was needed for me to snap out of it and start living in reality. Being emotionally fragile was no longer an excuse to invest my worth in the hands of men, in the hands of anyone for that matter. Despite feeling broken and discarded, my worth greeted me with no judgment or harshness. My worth allowed me to feel worthless before seeing the sun of my soul.

When I was ready to look myself in the eyes again without shame, and be OK with the reflection, choices and mistakes I had made—nothing else mattered. Emotional and spiritual growth was in my near future even if I couldn't yet see it.

My years of hurting happened and it was time to let the healing begin. No one could sway the goodness I had begun to find within myself. I was going to be just fine. Although it was hard to envision at first, the comfort of knowing that my joy was on the way, made me feel warm. There was so much potential ahead of me.

When I found myself...

I was laying in one piece on my bedroom floor which was flooded with tears of joy. My truth had been carved into my walls, with the pieces from my once shattered mirror that I learned to face daily. Through all of the crying and cracks in the glass I was finally learning how to put myself together for the very first time.

I'm thankful for my struggle because without it, I wouldn't
have stumbled across my strength.

-Day of Thanks

Who knew that after all of these years I'm still me without
you...It still shocks me to know that you are not
my life line; you are not my reason, my end or beginning.
It's nice to know now that you are my past.
Thank you for leaving me where you left me.
I appreciate you for ripping my heart into shreds, while forcing
me to drown in my own sorrow — I needed that...but I didn't
need you.

-Lessons from an Old Lover

I am still me without you.

I found myself in the same darkness that I found my light.

-Triumphant

I once wished for you, dreamt of you.

I loved you before seeing your face.

-Mine Now

Before I love you, I will love me 10 times greater.

And before I can want you, I have to experience the dying need of wanting my heart to beat in sync with how I breathe.

Please don't expect much from me when I can't clearly dust away the cobwebs from my past.

I'm yearning for our future but I have to learn what life is like without depending on a man.

-Co-dependent

Sadness doesn't live here but sometimes she visits.

-Go Home

Daddy Issues: 3

I've grown a lot.

I've forgiven my father.

I've found a man and I love him.

Hurting forever will only delay healing.

I am in charge of my life.

I take full responsibility for my happiness.

Not all men are like my father.

I no longer blame him for not knowing how to raise me

because at the end of the day I was uplifted by a Queen and she

taught me how to love me.

Gentle Reminder: 2

We owe ourselves a chance to try. Practice standing still and receiving the love that's being prepared for you. We can't get the love we want by running after it. Let love come to you.

I am the ocean and because of that

you can be my moon any day.

Your light is something I enjoy.

The kisses of warm that you leave on my blues allows our

reflections to intertwine, mix and mingle, glow and shine.

I'm so glad you're here even when you try to use the

clouds to hide.

-Exchange Reflections

Leaving will never be easy

but loving him will always be.

He gives love a new definition in my book; he speaks

my language.

-All Ways

I will never love you more than I love me.

That wouldn't be fair to either of us.

- True Love

He tried to run from me

but my love stopped him in his tracks.

He was halfway gone until he decided to look back.

-Stay

How did I forget who I was
but remember your name?
How did I extinguish my light
but ignite your flame?

-Selfless

Regularly I Close my eyes and See someone that I have yet to touch. He is what love looks like to me.

-Initials

He carries his energy in his hair.

His strands are powerful; they hang to his waist when he's

feeling free. I want to touch them, soak up his pride, and

intertwine in his glory and love him as long as

his locs latitude.

-Mane

You run, I follow. In the same breath when you trip,
I fall; right to your feet.

-Second Chances

Despite how hard things may get and regardless of how uncomfortable I may feel, quitting isn't an option. If my heart is in it I'm not giving up.

-Continue

Show me love, I don't want to hear it. I'm a visual learner.

-Demonstrate

I woke up with what seemed to be honey on my tongue.
Dreams of you are sweet, pleasant and savored until
the last drop.

-Taste

Maybe I should've become friends

with the noose of words

that he'd constantly hang me from...

It's almost like I loved the abuse.

-Dysfunction

There is a lump in my throat full of tears
but all this pride won't let the dam break.

-Flood

You know me better than I know myself. So much so
that you make my reflection nervous.
You figured out early on that my spirit is scenic...
 I'm glad you took the long way while getting to know me.

-Adventure

Rise in Light

I hope you rise with kindness on your tongue, love in your heart and forgiveness within your spirit. Today is a new day to be a better and more patient person than yesterday.

When I learned to think before speaking my words started to make more sense and they settled in the hearts of others softly.

-Careful

I am coated in sweetness

because a little less than forever ago

I was too sour to stomach my damn self.

There was no honey here...

My jar was empty.

I was bitter like jasmine tea that's been steeped too long.

My love was lost but I found it where I found my light.

-Glowing

If I didn't have you I would melt into a pile of nothingness.

You are the waves to my tide

and we all need water to survive.

-Sustain

I had to drown in my own tears

just to stay afloat.

There is a piece of me that can still

taste the salt on my lips from

the oceans that my eyes have poured out.

I have never been so happy to have survived such unhappiness.

-High Water

Is it selfish to ask for time back that
 I was granted to build
such a beautiful memory?

-Indian Giver

Our language is special.

Every time we open our mouths love spills out in abundance.

-Native Tongue

Gentle Reminder: 3

I deserve to be happy even if no one else around me understands where I've found my happiness.

I am the voice of the women who are
scared to speak up, who are ashamed of their
flaws and uncertain of their dreams.

-Bound Together

Hurt happens but so does healing.

Pick up your pieces and repair your peace.

-You Are Not Broken

I want to lay on you.

Please, lie to me not while I lay there.

-Truthful

Let us teach our young men to cry more.

Why is it not OK for a man to shed tears when his heart is full?

-Emote

The Sun will rise and set regardless.

What we choose to do with the light while it's here is up to us.

-Journey Wisely

Fear isn't allowed to run things over here.

Worry is destined to wither while sitting on my windowsill...

Being terrified to try won't torment me and

my past is no longer allowed to punish me for my

shortcomings; I will be great.

I am determined to be driven...

Nothing can stop my show; I've come too far to fumble the

dreams that belong to me.

-Bold

I have never known happiness like this.

I feel warm, comforted and wrapped up in a
vibration of joy.

There is no language that can describe this love.

-The Love of Self

The following pages are for you to enjoy.

Write your language.

-Alex Elle

Title:

Title:

Title:

Title:

Title:

Title:

Title:

Title:

Title:

43876087R00122

Made in the USA
Lexington, KY
15 August 2015